Embroidery pour la Maison

Many thanks to:

Solange, for the lovely fabrics we've used in this book. They're for sale in the charming notions shop, Salon Aiguilles, in Vincennes (94).
Thierry, who has a gift for bringing out the best in everything he photographs, with or without that delicious Speculoos spread.
DMC, for the beautiful embroidery threads that they so generously provided.
Julie Wullems, for her invaluable assistance.
And all my love to Christine, for her unfailing trust and kindness.

Original edition: copyright © 2011 by Fleurus Editions
English translation: copyright © 2013 by HarperCollins Publishers

HarperCollins books may be purchased for educational, business, or sales promotional use. For information please write:
Special Markets Department, HarperCollins Publishers, 10 East 53rd Street, New York, NY 10022.

Published in 2013 by:
Harper Design
An Imprint of HarperCollins*Publishers*
10 East 53rd Street
New York, NY 10022
Tel (212) 207-7000
harperdesign@harpercollins.com
www.harpercollins.com

Distributed throughout the world by:
HarperCollins Publishers
10 East 53rd Street
New York, NY 10022

Library of Congress Control Number: 2012947749

ISBN: 978-0-06-222261-9

Printed in China, 2012

Embroidery, designs, and fabrication: Sylvie Blondeau
Interior font design: Arnoldas Dambrauskas
Photographs: Thierry Antablian
Editorial direction: Guillaume Pô
Editing: Christine Hooghe
Artistic direction: Isabelle Mayer
Production: Sabine Marioni
Translation: Elizabeth G. Heard

Embroidery pour la Maison

100 French Designs for the Home

Sylvie Blondeau

HARPER DESIGN

An Imprint of HarperCollins Publishers

Brodez la vie!

A piece of linen, a few strands of thread, and a needle—these are the only supplies you need to start embroidering! Pages 52 through 59 of this book break down all the stitches you need to know to create feminine touches for the things you use every day; because all your things should be beautiful. It's life's little pleasures that do so much good for us: indulging in girl-talk with friends over a cup of tea, enjoying a leisurely bubble bath, trying on an airy summer frock . . . and this book gives you an array of designs to personalize your accessories with reminders of these. There's even an extra bonus: a tasty cupcake recipe to savor as you stitch.

APPLE PIE.

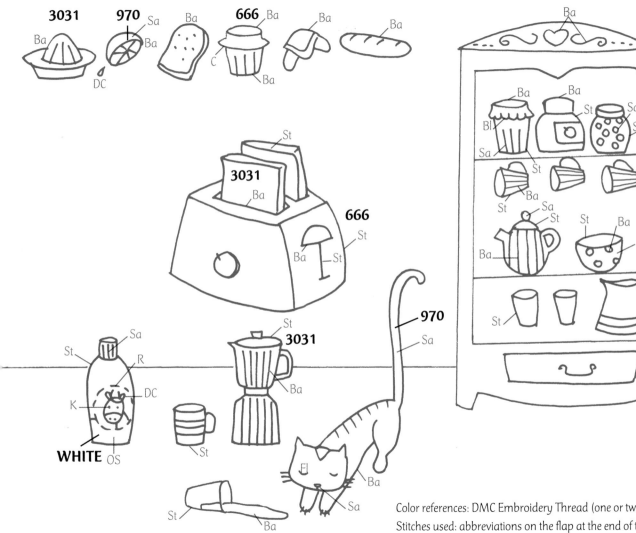

3031

970 Sa
Ba

Ba

Ba
DC

666 Ba

Ba
C
Ba

Ba

Ba

Ba

Ba
Bl
Sa
Sa

Ba
St
Sa
St

St
Sa
St

St
Ba

St

St
Sa
St

St
Ba

Ba

Sa

St

Ba

St

St

St

3031
LS
3821

Ba

K

Ba

St

666

Ba

St

3031
Ba

St

666

St
St
Ba

St
Sa
R

DC

K

WHITE OS

St
Sa
3031

Ba

St
970
Sa

El

Ba

Sa

St
Ba

Color references: DMC Embroidery Thread (one or two strands, depending on the photograph).
Stitches used: abbreviations on the flap at the end of the book, instructions on pages 54–59.

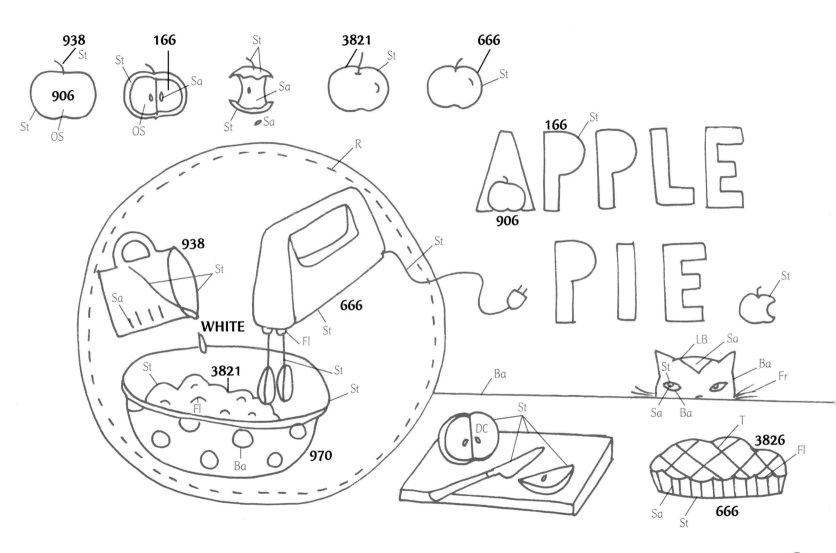

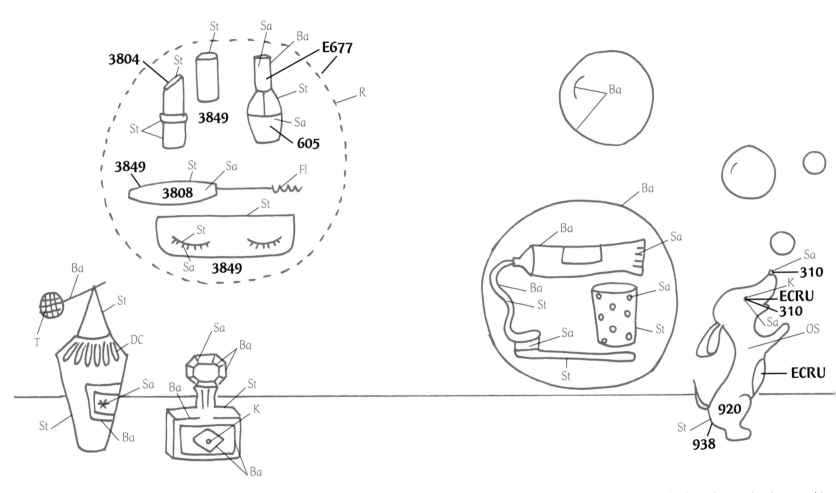

Color references: DMC Embroidery Thread (one or two strands, depending on the photograph).
Stitches used: abbreviations on the flap at the end of the book, instructions on pages 54–59.

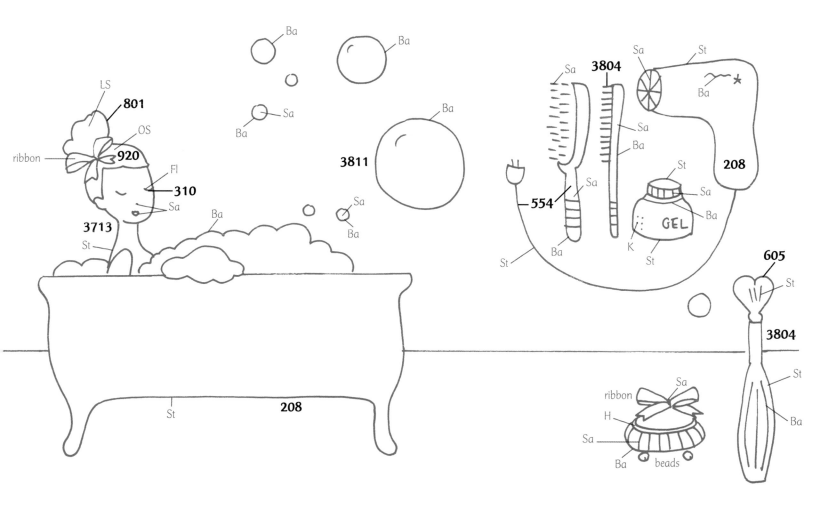

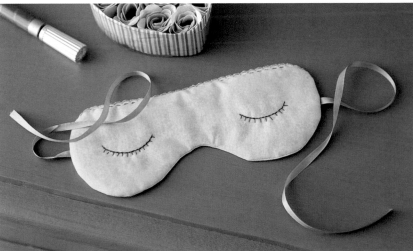

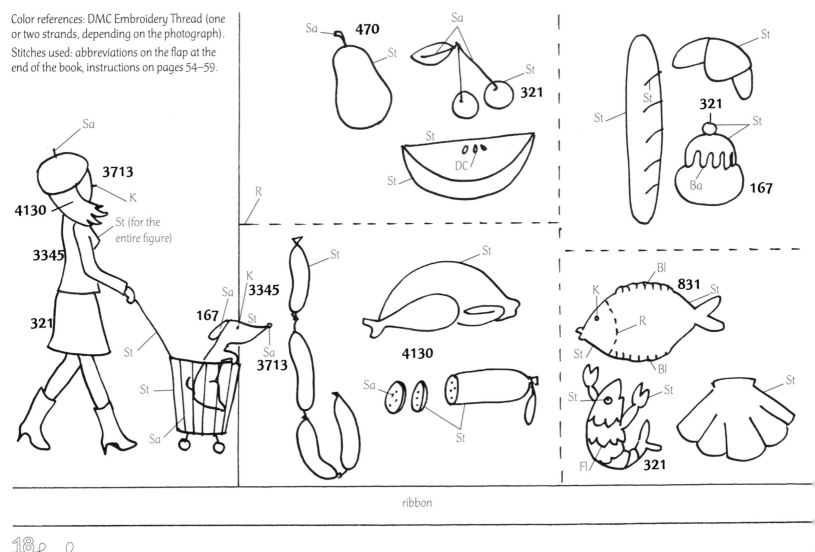

Color references: DMC Embroidery Thread (one or two strands, depending on the photograph).

Stitches used: abbreviations on the flap at the end of the book, instructions on pages 54–59.

ribbon

18

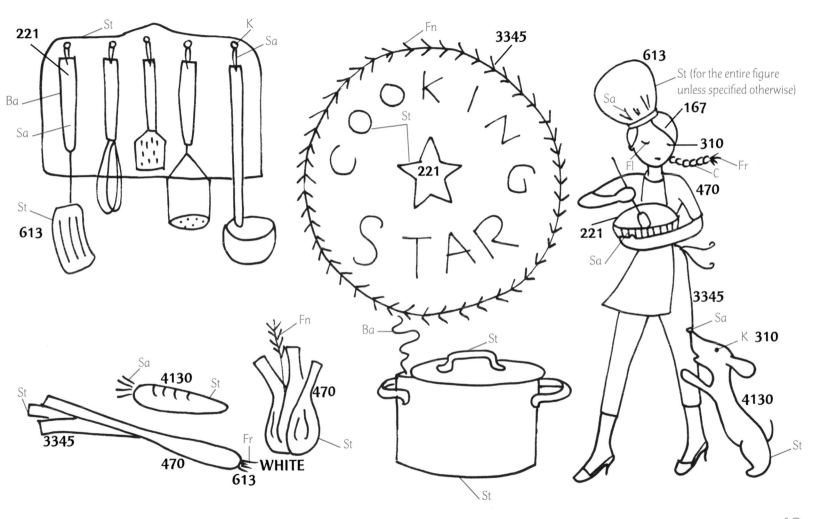

COOKING STAR

19

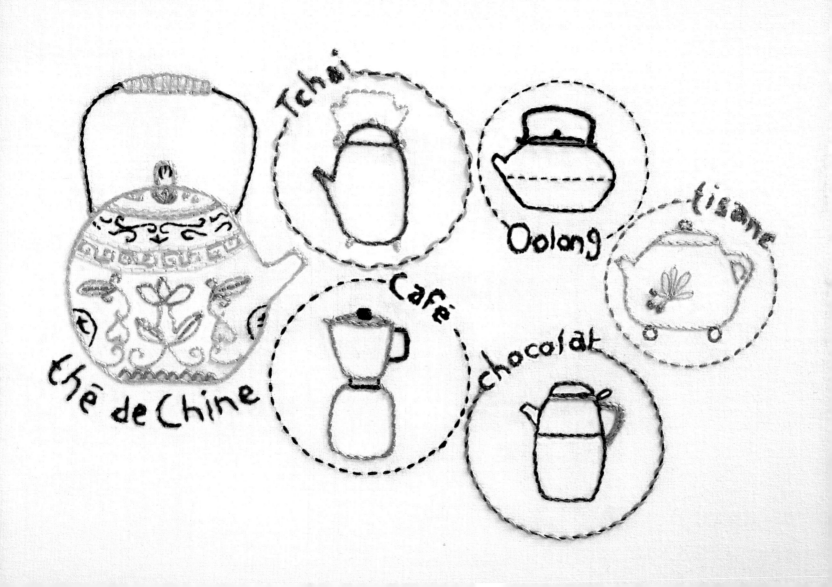

Tchaï

Oolong

tisane

thé de Chine

Café

chocolat

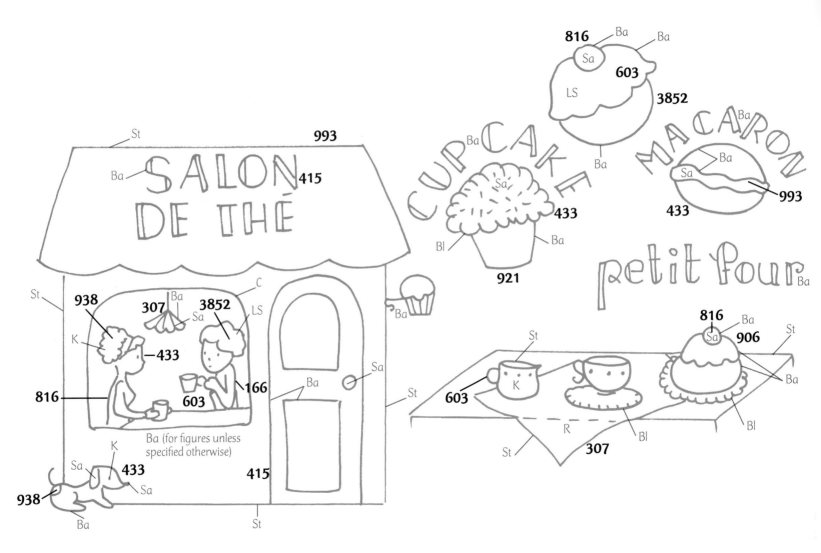

SALON DE THÉ

CUP CAKE

MACARON

petit four

Ba (for figures unless specified otherwise)

22

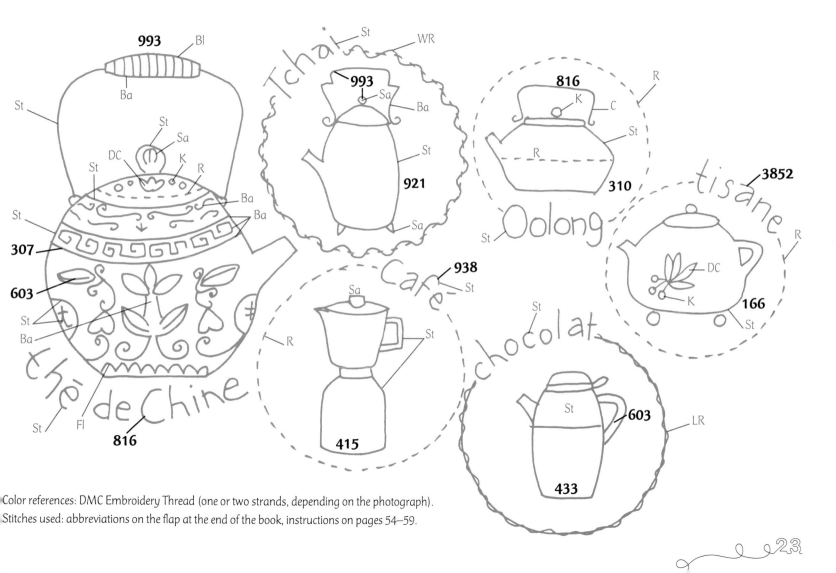

993 Bl
Ba
St
St
DC
Sa
St
R
St
K
Ba
St
Ba
307
603
St
Ba
St
Fl
816
thé de Chine

Tchai St
WR
993
Sa
Ba
St
921
Sa
Café 938
St
Sa
R
St
415
Oolong St

816
K
C
R
St
R
310
chocolat
St
St
603
LR
433

tisane 3852
R
DC
K
166
St

Color references: DMC Embroidery Thread (one or two strands, depending on the photograph).
Stitches used: abbreviations on the flap at the end of the book, instructions on pages 54–59.

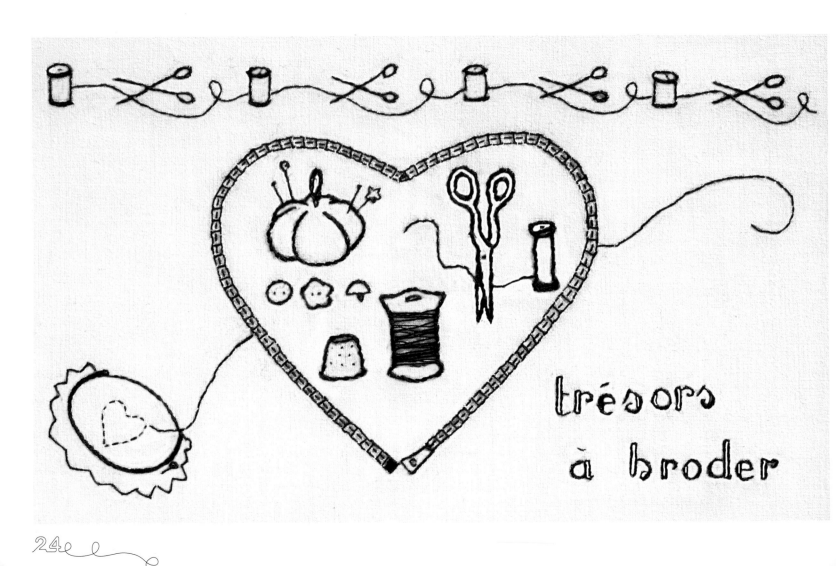

trésors
à broder

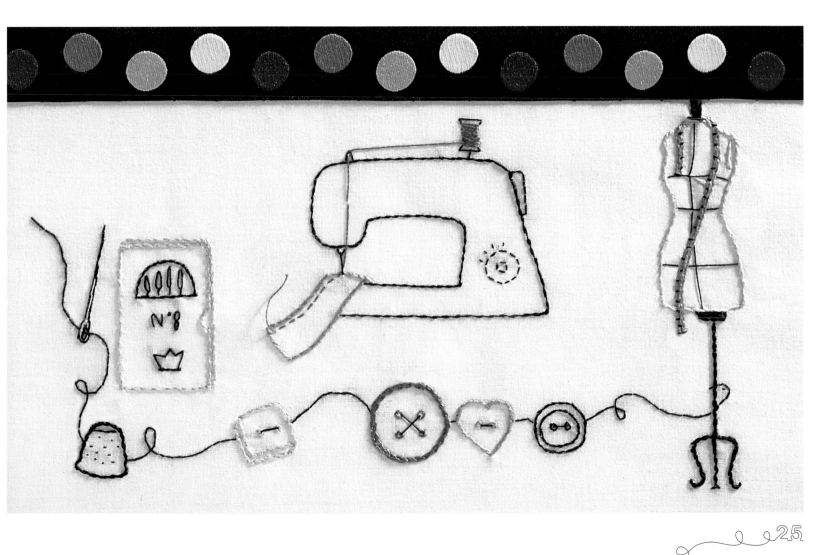

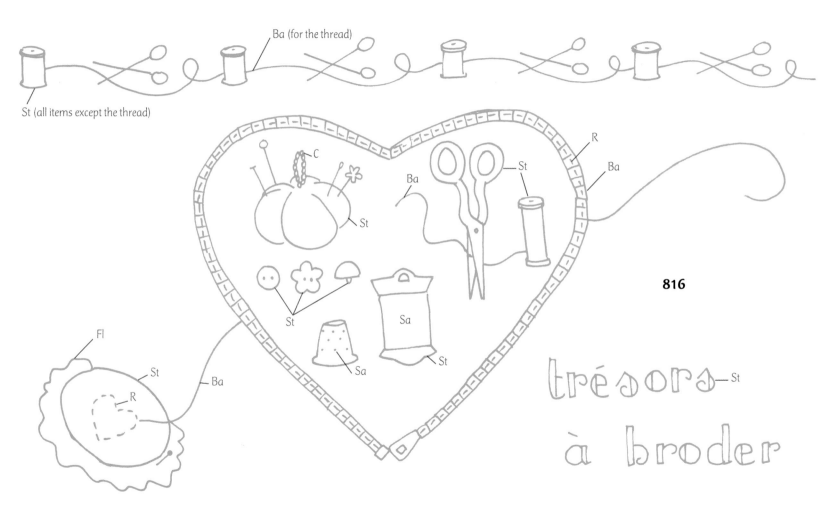

Ba (for the thread)

St (all items except the thread)

C

St

Ba

R

Ba

St

Sa

St

Sa

St

Fl

St

R

Ba

816

trésors — St

à broder

26

Color references: DMC Embroidery Thread (one or two strands, depending on the photograph).

Stitches used: abbreviations on the flap at the end of the book, instructions on pages 54–59.

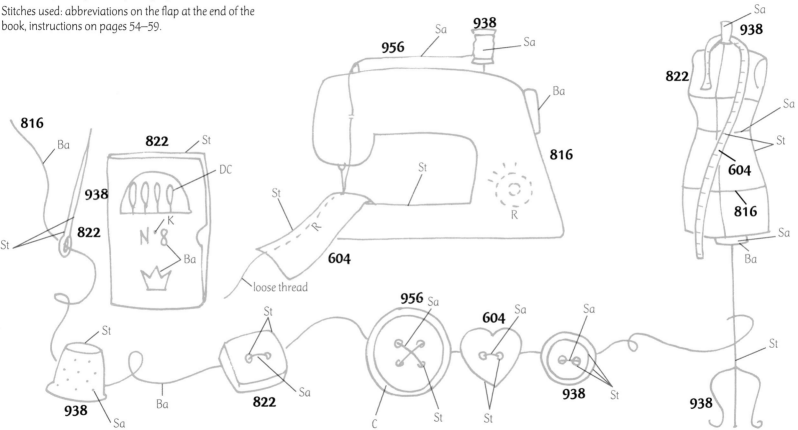

Tea caddy
designs page 22
instructions page 63

Placemat
designs page 22 (enlarged)
instructions page 63

Buttons
designs pages 9, 22, 37, and 40
instructions page 62

Sewing scissors charm
design page 23
instructions page 62

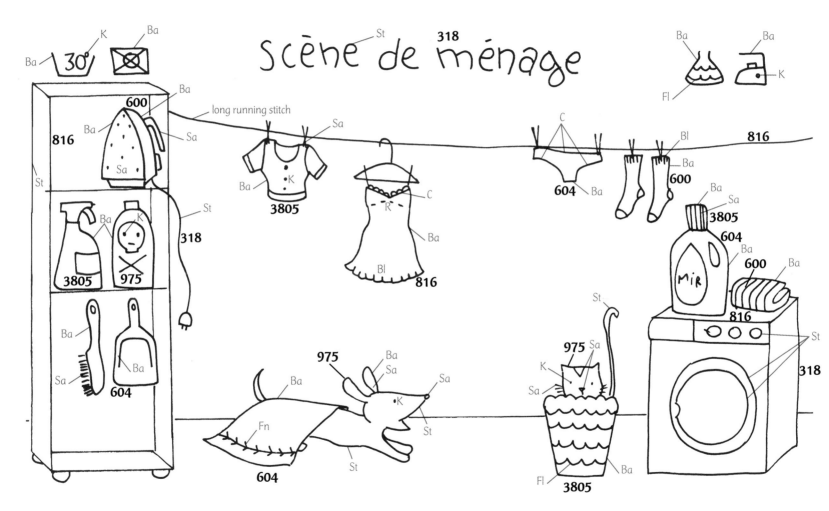

scène de ménage

Color references: DMC Embroidery Thread (one or two strands, depending on the photograph).
Stitches used: abbreviations on the flap at the end of the book, instructions on pages 54–59.

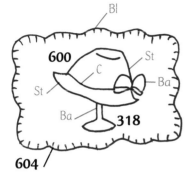

Bl
600
St
C
St
Ba
Ba
318
604

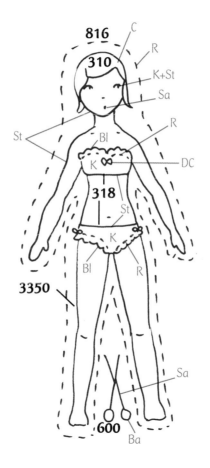

816
C
310
R
K+St
Sa
R
St
Bl
K
DC
318
St
K
Bl
R
3350
Sa
600
Ba

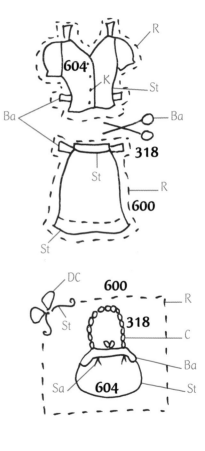

R
604
K
St
Ba
Ba
318
St
600
St
DC
600
R
St
318
C
Ba
Sa
604
St

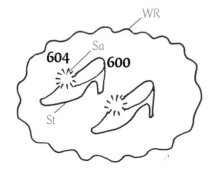

WR
Sa
604
600
St

33

34

Color references: DMC Embroidery Thread (one or two strands, depending on the photograph).
Stitches used: abbreviations on the flap at the end of the book, instructions on pages 54–59.

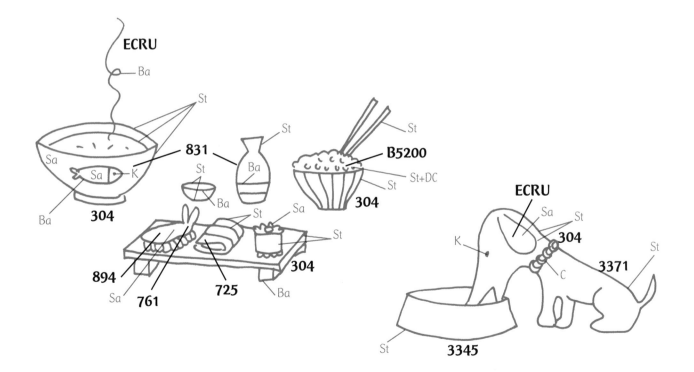

Food: all outlines in backstitch

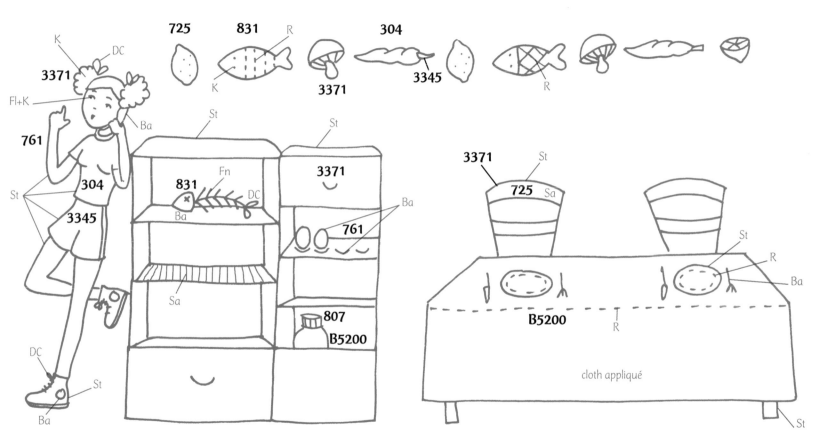

cloth appliqué

37

Recipe book
design page 19
instructions page 62

Tote bag
design page 13
instructions page 61

Cell phone case
design page 40
instructions page 61

Pencil case
design page 36
instructions page 61

TIC TOC

DRIING

ECOLE

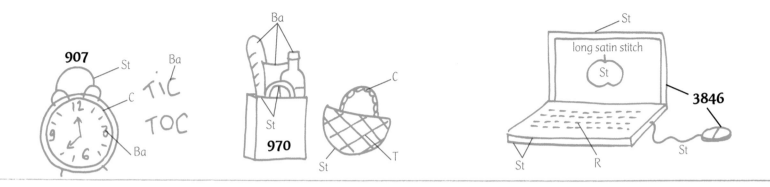

907 St Ba C TIC TOC C Ba

Ba Ba St 970 C St T

St long satin stitch St 3846 St R St

ribbon

 DRIING St Ba Ba K

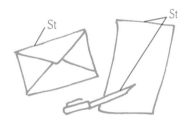 St St

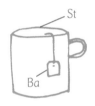 St Ba

R

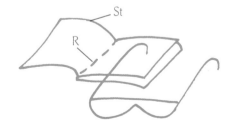 St R

 Ba

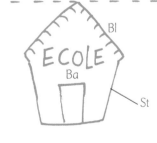 Bl ECOLE Ba St

K St Sa Fl

42

907 St

3846 Sa

970

307

cloth appliqué

R
St

St

Sa
167 K
Sa
St
Sa
St
Sa
St
St

St
DC
R
St
R
K

R
St
St

R
St
DC

Color references: DMC Embroidery Thread (one or two strands, depending on the photograph).
Stitches used: abbreviations on the flap at the end of the book, instructions on pages 54–59.

44

45

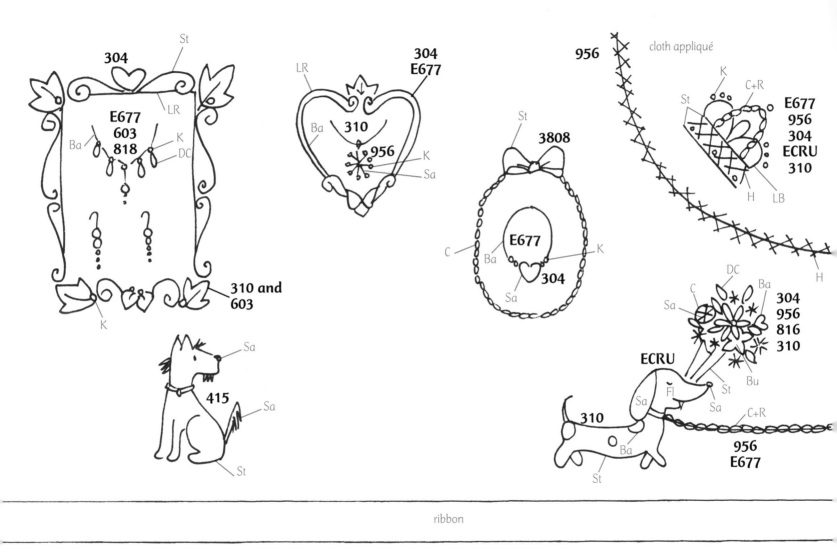

304

St

E677
603
818

Ba

K

DC

LR

310 and
603

K

304
E677

LR

Ba

310

956

K

Sa

956

cloth appliqué

St

K

C+R

E677
956
304
ECRU
310

H

LB

St

3808

E677

C

Ba

K

304

Sa

H

DC

C

Ba

Sa

304
956
816
310

St

Bu

ECRU

Sa

Fl

Sa

C+R

Sa

415

Sa

St

310

Ba

956
E677

St

ribbon

46

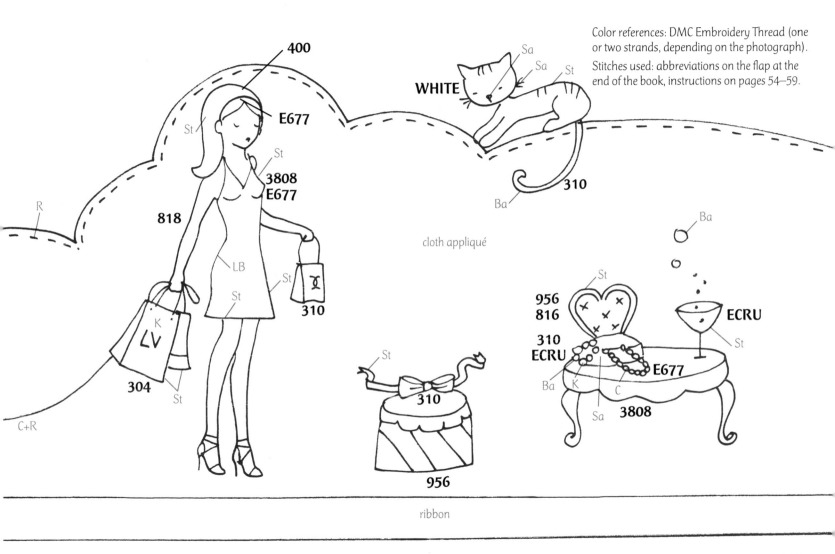

Color references: DMC Embroidery Thread (one or two strands, depending on the photograph).

Stitches used: abbreviations on the flap at the end of the book, instructions on pages 54–59.

400

E677

St

3808
E677

818

LB

St

St

K

LV

St

304

R

C+R

WHITE

Sa
Sa
St

310

Ba

cloth appliqué

St

310

956

Ba

956
816

310
ECRU

St

Ba K C

Sa

3808

E677

ECRU

St

ribbon

Address book
design page 40
instructions page 63

Lampshade
design page 33
instructions page 63

Change purse
design page 33
instructions page 62

Badges
design pages 33 and 42 (adjusted to the size of the backing)
instructions page 62

Gift bag
design page 47
instructions page 60

50

The embroiderer's recipe

The perfect cupcake

Ingredients
- 2 cups (240 g) flour
- ⅓ cup (75 g) small oat flakes
- 2 tsp. (1 packet) baking powder
- ½ cup (110 g) brown sugar
- 3 eggs
- ⅔ cup (150 ml) milk
- ½ cup (110 ml) sunflower oil or melted butter
- Ground cinnamon and ginger or allspice, 2 chopped apples tossed with lemon juice (optional)
- ⅔ cup (150 g) confectioner's sugar
- A few drops of lemon juice
- Food coloring
- Candies, marshmallows, sugar sprinkles, chocolate chips, fruit . . .

Cake batter
Preheat the oven to 400°F (205°C).

Combine the flour, oat flakes, baking powder, and brown sugar in a large bowl.

Combine the milk, sunflower oil or melted butter, and two eggs in another large bowl.

Add the liquid ingredients to the first bowl, being careful not to overmix the batter.

Add the spices or apples if you wish.

Pour batter into a cupcake pan and bake 15 to 20 minutes. Check doneness by testing with a toothpick (cook longer if necessary).

Icing and decoration
Separate the egg yolk from the white. Combine the confectioner's sugar and the egg white.

Add the lemon juice and coloring.

Spread on cupcakes and decorate as desired.

Chill for 30 minutes until the icing sets.

Enjoy!

Secrets of embroidery

Supplies

The fabric
As a beginner, it's best to use a fairly tightly woven cotton fabric in a pastel color. If you sew, you can have fun mixing and matching fabrics. You can also begin with fabric objects such as pillows, aprons, and tea towels.

Mechanical pencil and eraser
A regular pencil works perfectly for drawing designs on light-colored fabrics.

Embroidery hoop
It's not essential, but tightly stretched fabric helps make your stitches more regular.

Embroidery needles
They have an elongated eye and nicely sharp points. Number 9 needles are perfect.

Embroidery scissors
Their short blades cut threads very close to the fabric surface, so there's no risk of losing control!

DMC Embroidery Threads
are available in more than 450 colors. The range includes metallic threads (Light Effects) and shaded threads (Color Variations). The floss consists of six easily separated strands. The embroidery designs in this book generally use one or two strands depending on the desired thickness.

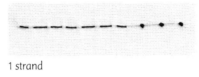

1 strand

2 strands

3 strands

4 strands

Start out right!

Transfer the design
Photocopy the design you have chosen in the desired size, or trace it.

Using tracing paper, trace the design with a pencil onto carefully ironed fabric. You can tape the design and the fabric to a window to increase transparency.

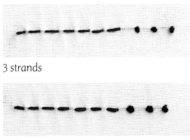

For dark-colored fabrics, you can buy special embroidery transfer pencils or carbon paper at a notions shop.

Stretch the fabric (if you want to . . .)
Place the fabric between the two rings of the embroidery hoop with the screw loosened.

Place the rings together and tighten the screw, pulling the fabric around the hoop if necessary.

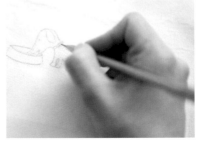

Thread the needle

Pull on the end of the skein.

Cut off a piece 12 to 16 inches (30 to 40 cm) long.

Separate as many strands as you need.

Slide the thread through the eye. It's easier if you moisten it.

Start embroidering

Without making a knot in the thread, bring the needle up through the outline of the design, and then pull it through, leaving

about ½ inch (1 or 2 cm) of thread hanging down underneath. Continue embroidering, securing the end of the thread beneath your next few stitches.

Finishing off

To end a piece of thread, run it beneath the last few stitches. Snip off the end of the thread so it is flush with the fabric.

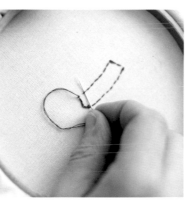

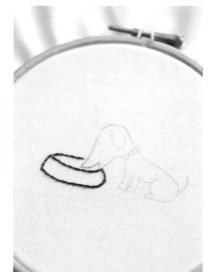

Follow that thread!

Now you know the basics. Practice with a simple outline stitch (the following pages will help you), then gradually begin experimenting with other stitches. Play with the scale of the designs, or add ribbons, beads, buttons, and even fabric appliqués: just fold under the raw edge of the fabric all around, then sew it on with tiny stitches.

A collection of stitches

Use the simplest outline stitches in pretty colors, and you'll start making beautiful things right away! The selection below will help you try out new effects and have even more fun. The stitches used in the models are indicated by abbreviations next to them. The alphabetical list of these abbreviations printed on the flap at the back of the book will be a useful reference.

Outline stitches

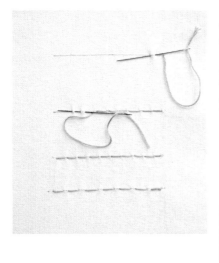

Running stitch (R)

Working from right to left, pass the needle through the fabric in an up-and-down motion at regular intervals. For an almost continuous line, leave only one or two threads in the fabric weave between each stitch. For a looser look, space the stitches farther apart.

Helpful hint

The direction given for these stitches is for a right-handed person. If you're left-handed, look at the diagrams in a mirror.

Backstitch (Ba)

Worked from right to left, as its name suggests, this stitch embroiders from front to back. Make short, regular stitches, as close together as possible.

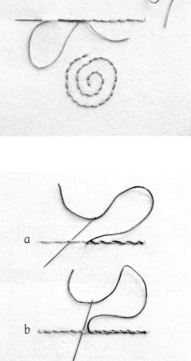

Laced running stitch (LR) or Laced backstitch (LB)

Embroider a line in running stitch (a) or backstitch (b). Lace another thread from top to bottom over each stitch you've already made.

a

b

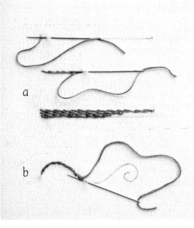

Stem stitch (St)

Work from left to right, and bring the needle up halfway back behind each stitch while keeping the loop of thread below the needle. Arranged in side-by-side lines, this stitch can be used to fill in forms (a). To follow curved lines perfectly, combine the "backward" variation of the stem stitch with the traditional version of the stem stitch. Proceed in the same fashion, but keeping the thread above the needle (b).

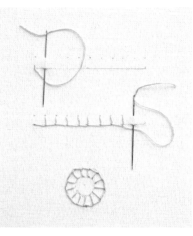

Blanket stitch (Bl)

This stitch can be used for straight lines, curves, or circles (wheels), working from left to right. Insert the needle into the fabric above the line and bring it through on the line, keeping the thread to the right. Space the stitches regularly.

Chain stitch (C)

This stitch can be used to outline or fill in. Work from top to bottom. Make regular loops by passing the thread under the needle with each stitch. Finish the last loop with a small straight stitch.

Buttonhole stitch (Bu)

This stitch is done like the blanket stitch but with the stitches more closely spaced.

Detached stitches

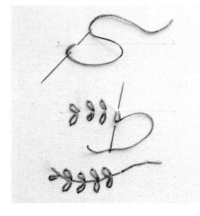

Detached chain stitch (DC)
Do this stitch like a chain stitch, securing each loop individually with a straight stitch, using the length appropriate for the desired effect.

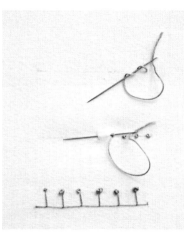

Knot stitch (K)
Bring the needle up through the fabric. With your left hand roll the thread one, two, or three times in tight loops around the needle. While still holding the thread, insert the needle back down into the fabric in the same spot where you brought the needle up. Pull the thread, sliding the loops off. The knot is now formed.

Fringe (Fr)
This stitch is used for animal whiskers, the ends of pigtails, etc. Leave the thread on the front of the fabric, and make two little stitches one on top of the other. Then cut, leaving the end of the thread loose. Repeat as necessary.

Filling stitches

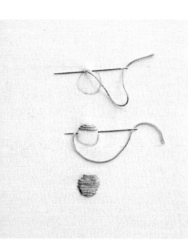

Satin stitch (Sa)
This stitch is most frequently used to fill in small areas. Bring the needle up at the edge of the area to be covered and bring the thread all the way across it, inserting the needle back down on the opposite edge of the design. On the reverse side, bring the needle back up right next to where you began the preceding stitch. Align the stitches to create the desired effect. You can also space them further apart or use them individually.

Long and short stitch (LS)
Embroider a row of vertical satin stitches, alternating short and long stitches. Then, working in the opposite direction, make satin stitches of the same length under the short stitches. Continue over the entire area of the design. This stitch is ideal for covering larger surfaces and allows you to create lovely color shading effects.

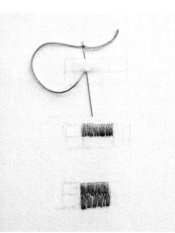

Overlapping satin stitch (OS)
Embroider a row of vertical satin stitches. For the second and additional rows, bring the needle up between two stitches of the preceding row; the rows will overlap each other.

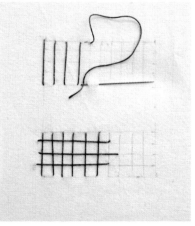

Trellis (T)
Embroider a series of regularly spaced stitches, and then another set perpendicular to the first, interweaving each stitch with those in the first series before inserting the needle back into the fabric.

Borders and edgings

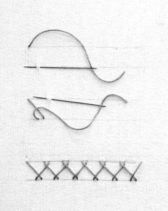

Herringbone stitch (H)

This stitch is executed in two parallel lines. Bring the needle up to the upper line. Take a small straight stitch from right to left, inserting the needle back down at the lower line. Take another small straight stitch on the lower line. Then make another small straight stitch on the upper line. Space the stitches evenly.

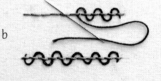

Whipped running stitch (WR)

Embroider a line of running stitches (a) or backstitches (b). Lace a second thread up and down through the stitches already made, creating the effect of a wave.

Fly stitch (Fl)

This stitch is done from left to right, in lines, overlapping lines, or individually. Bring the needle up to the left of the line and insert it into the fabric as if making a straight stitch, forming a V-shaped loop without pulling too hard on the thread. Bring the needle up again farther down, in the middle of the stitch, and make a vertical straight stitch to secure the previous stitch.

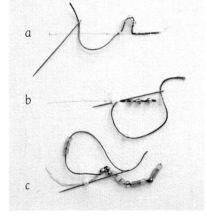

Beading (Be)

Depending on your design, there are a number of ways to attach the beads:
- running stitch (a)
- backstitch (b)
- combination of running stitch and backstitch (c)

Fern stitch (Fn)

Begin at the top of the line. Make three running stitches of the same length, forming an angle between them and inserting the needle through the same hole at the base of each of the three stitches. To continue the design, make the next stitch just below the first and continue in the same way.

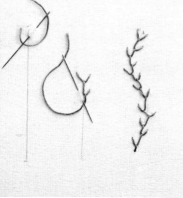

Feather stitch (Fe)

Bring the needle up at the top of the line, then alternate to the left and right, always keeping the needle above the length of thread.

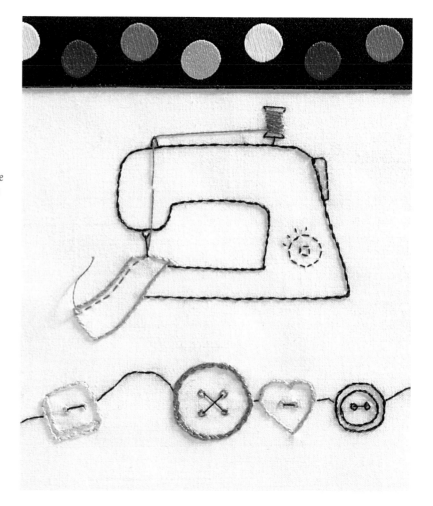

Instructions

Embroidering is terrific fun, and showcasing your creations on decorative and useful objects is doubly satisfying. The projects in this book are designed for both new and experienced embroiderers, and they can also be a source of inspiration for you. Feel free to embroider any design you like on something store-bought or hand-made. Customize the colors, fine-tune the dimensions—personalize however you please!

To keep the instructions simple, only the specific supplies and the sewing steps needed for each project are given. Seam allowances are included. For the embroidery designs, refer to the photographs and design pages. For a professional quality finish, match the thread colors, oversew the pieces of fabric, and flatten the seams with an iron as you go along.

Bags, purses, and such

Assorted drawstring bags

Supplies
For each bag: Two different fabrics (one for the bottom, the other for the lining and reverse), ribbon, braid.
Seam allowance: ¼ inch (0.5 cm).

1 Cut two squares of fabric for the bottom depending on the size of bag you've decided to make: 5½ x 5½ inches (14 x 14 cm), 7 x 7 inches (18 x 18 cm) or 9¾ x 9¾ inches (25 x 25 cm). Round off two corners. For the lining, cut two rectangles measuring 5½ x 7½ inches (14 x 19 cm), 7 x 9 inches (18 x 23 cm) or 9¾ x 11¾ inches (25 x 30 cm). Again, round off two corners.

2 Embroider the design on one side. Lay the two side pieces on top of each other, right sides in. Sew the bottom and sides together.

Turn right side out. Sew the lining leaving a ⅜ to ¾ inch (1 cm to 2 cm) opening on top of one of the sides.

3 Put the lining inside the bag, right sides facing in. Fold it up ¼ inch (0.5 cm) then fold it down 1¾ inches (4.5 cm) on the bag. Overstitch all around the bag, from one side of the opening to the other. Attach the braid below the lining by stitching through the entire thickness. Slide the ribbon through the drawstring casing.

Gift bag

Supplies
Two different fabrics, unbleached linen, ribbon.
Seam allowance: ¼ inch (0.5 cm).

1 Cut three rectangles: one 7½ x 6 inches (19 x 15 cm) from the linen, one 7½ x 1¾ inches (19 x 3.5 cm), and another of 7½ x 2 inches (19 x 5 cm) from the fabric. Sew them

right sides facing in; you'll have a rectangle measuring 7½ x 8¾ inches (19 x 22.5 cm). Embroider the design on the lower part of the linen, centering it.

2 Cut out a circle 2½ inches (6 cm) in diameter from the bottom piece of fabric. Right sides facing in, sew the rectangle around the circular opening, then sew the sides of the rectangle. Turn right side out.

3 Apply the other rectangular strip above and secure it with blanket stitches. Close with a ribbon.

Laundry bag

Supplies
Fabric, unbleached linen, bias binding.
Seam allowance: ¼ inch (0.5 cm).

1 Cut out two rectangles measuring 12½ x 11¾ inches (32 x 30 cm) from the fabric and a rectangle of 12½ x 13¾ inches (32 x 35 cm) from the linen. Fold over the short side of the linen and mark the fold at the bottom of the bag. Embroider the design on the side.

2 Place the linen between the two rectangles of fabric, right sides facing in. Fold the strip you have made, right sides facing in, and sew the sides, stopping 5½ inches (14 cm) from the top.

3 Cut out the rounded areas at the top, then cut a scoop to create the handles, referring to the diagram on page 64. Sew the top of the handles. Turn right side out.

4 For the label, use a linen rectangle measuring about 1½ x 4¾ inches (4 x 12 cm), folding the long sides ¼ inch (0.5 cm) over toward the center of the strip. Fold over the short sides. The design should go above the fold (embroider it before cutting the fabric).

5 Pin the label on the front. Sew the bias binding all around the opening and the handles.

Tote bag

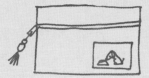

Supplies
Fabric, unbleached linen, oilcloth.
Seam allowance: ½ inch (1 cm).

1 Cut out a 9¾ x 6 inch (25 x 15 cm) rectangle from the linen and embroider the design ½ inch (1 cm) above the lower edge. Cut out a 10½ x 11¾ inch (27 x 30 cm) rectangle from the fabric. Sew together the linen and the fabric, right sides facing in.

2 Fold the strip you have made, right sides facing in, and sew the sides of the bag. At each corner, open the bottom of the bag by overlapping the central fold and the side seam. Sew a seam perpendicular to the side seam 1¼ inch (3 cm) from the corner.

3 For the lining, cut two 10½ x 17 inch (27 x 43 cm) strips of oilcloth and sew in the same way, leaving a 4 inch (10 cm) opening on one of the sides. Turn right side out.

4 For the handles, cut two 2 x 7¾ inch (5 x 20 cm) strips of fabric. Fold them in half, right sides facing in, and sew the long side. Turn right side out.

5 Place the lining, right side facing in, inside the bag. Insert the handles 2¾ inches (7 cm) from the side seams. Sew the top of the bag. Go back to the opening. Close.

Cell phone or glasses case

Supplies
Two fabrics (one for the exterior, the other for the lining), unbleached linen, ribbon. Seam allowance: ¼ inch (0.5 cm).

This is made of a long strip of lined fabric that's folded to form the two sides of a little case with a flap for fastening. Feel free to adapt the measurements to the size of your cell phone or glasses. Final dimensions, with the flap: 2 ½ x 3 ¼ inch (6.5 x 8 cm).

1 Cut a 1¾ x 3½ inch (4.5 x 9 cm) rectangle from the linen and embroider the design. On either side, sew a ¾ x 3½ inch (2 x 9 cm) strip of fabric, right sides facing in. For the back and the flap, cut a 2¾ x 4¾ inch (7.5 x 12 cm) strip. With right sides facing in, line up one of the shorter sides at the base of the front. Sew. Round off the corners of the flap.

2 Arrange the assembled pieces on the liner fabric, right sides facing in, and cut out a piece of identical size. Sew all around, leaving a 1½ inch (4 cm) opening. Turn right side out.

3 Fold the case over. Sew the sides with the overcast stitch, attaching a loop of ribbon. Fold down the flap and iron flat. Variation: if you like, you can add a snap closure, a piece of Velcro, or a decorative button with a little embroidered button loop.

Pencil holder

Supplies
Oilcloth (in two colors), unbleached linen, protective plastic sheeting, 7¾ inch (20 cm) zipper.
Seam allowance: ½ inch (1 cm).

1 From the oilcloth, cut a 8¾ x 6¾ inch (22 x 17 cm) rectangle (for the back and upper part of the front) and a 8¾ x 4¼ inch (22 x 11 cm) rectangle (for the front).

2 Embroider the design on the linen. Cut around if necessary and appliqué this piece to the front, using straight or zigzag stitches, covering it with a piece of plastic of the same size.

3 Fold in one of the long sides of each oilcloth rectangle ¼ inch (0.5 cm) and oversew it to the zipper. Open the zipper and turn the pencil case inside out. Stitch the three sides. Crimp the edges of the seams at the corners. Turn right side out. If you wish, you can add a personal touch to the zipper with ribbon, beads, or a fancy tassel.

Change purse

Supplies
Two types of fabric (exterior and lining), metal clasp.

1 Make the purse: Trace the exterior outline of the metal clasp onto paper. Using this as a model, draw the desired size of the purse. Cut out the pattern and trace it two times on each piece of fabric, adding ¼ inch (0.5 cm) as a seam allowance all around. Cut out each piece.

2 With right sides facing in, sew the exterior pieces together up to the level of the clasp, then do the same with the lining pieces. Place the lining inside the purse, right side facing in. Sew the two layers to the edge of the clasp. Attach them to the clasp. Then spread open the groove of the clasp and push the fabric into this opening.

Accessories

Eye mask

Supplies
Fabric, flannel, lace or braid.
Seam allowance: ¼ inch (0.5 cm).

1 Draw the shape on a 4 x 9 inch (10 x 23 cm) paper rectangle, referring to the diagram on page 64. Trace it twice on the fabric and once on the flannel. Embroider the design.

2 Place the fabric shapes, right sides facing in, on the felt. On each side, insert a 20 inch (50 cm) piece of ribbon. Sew the sides and the bottom.

3 Turn the piece right side out. Close the opening by folding it in and sewing a piece of lace or braid between the two pieces of fabric.

Buttons

Supplies
Buttons to be covered, unbleached linen, or fabric.

1 Embroider the design on the fabric. Trace a circle of the diameter specified by the button manufacturer. Cut out. Stitch around a gathering thread.

2 Center the button on the fabric circle. Gather and tie the thread. Attach the button as instructed.

Badges

Proceed as with the buttons, choosing larger backings. Depending on the model, it may be necessary to cut off the bottom with pincers and paste the two parts of the button together. Then glue a pin to the back.

If you use a badge-making machine, increase the seam allowances specified by the manufacturer and again use a gathering thread. The fabric will then stay in place during the production process.

Embroidery scissors charm

Supplies
Fabric, unbleached linen, padding, narrow ribbon.

Embroider the design on the fabric. Cut it in a square measuring about 2¾ inches (7 cm) on each side. Cut out an identical square of linen. Sew them together right side facing in, about ¼ inch (0.5 cm) from the edges, inserting a ribbon folded in half in the corner and leaving an opening on one side. Turn right side out. Insert padding. Sew together with small stitches.

Recipe book

Supplies
Two types of fabric (one for the exterior, the other for the lining), unbleached linen, 2 ribbons (one wide with a decorative design and the other narrow), a notebook.
Seam allowance: ¼ inch (0.5 cm).

1 Place the open notebook on the two pieces of fabric. Add 2 inches (5 cm) to each side and ½ inch (1 cm) on the top and bottom. Cut out.

2 Embroider the design on the linen, then sew it onto the front of the cover. Embroider the design on the bookmark. Turn under the rough edge all around and hand sew it to the liner fabric, prepared in the same way, inserting a ribbon.

3 Sew the cover fabrics, right sides facing in, leaving a 2 inch (5 cm) opening (on the back side) and inserting a ribbon bookmark on top, in the center. Turn right side out. Close the opening. Sew on the embroidered ribbon.

4 Fold the flaps over 1½ inches (4 cm). Oversew the top and bottom of the notebook or just sew the flaps using the overcast stitch.

Address book

Make it just like the recipe notebook, but with only one type of fabric (for the lining and exterior). The length corresponds to that of the book and the flaps are hand-sewn on the top and bottom. The embroidery and beads are applied before sewing.

Home décor

Placemat

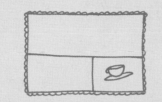

Supplies
Two types of fabric, unbleached linen, braid or lace for trimming.
Seam allowance: ¼ inch (0.5 cm).

1 Cut two 6¾ x 4¼ inch (17 x 11 cm) rectangles of fabric and linen and a 13 x 6 inch (33 x 15 cm) rectangle of a different fabric. Embroider the design on the linen.

2 Sew the two rectangular pieces side by side together by one of the shorter sides. Sew them to the third rectangle.

3 Fold the edges in ¼ inch (0.5 cm) all the way around. Hem by hand using the running stitch for the trim.

Tea caddy

Supplies
Two types of fabric, unbleached linen, felt, binding.
The size suggested on page 64 is for a 7 inch (18 cm) teapot that holds one liter.

1 Draw a pattern on paper. Try it on your teapot. Adjust if necessary. Cut a piece of linen two times for the top and a piece of fabric two times for the bottom, adding a ½ inch (1 cm) seam allowance. Embroider the design on the linen.

2 Sew the top and bottom of each side together. Using one side as a pattern, cut out two matching pieces of felt.

3 For the decorative handle on top, sew two 2¾ x 4¼ inch (7 x 11 cm) rectangles of cloth together, right sides facing in, leaving an opening. Turn right side out and close the opening. Fold 5½ inch (14 cm) of binding in half and make a 1¼ inch (3 cm) seam in the loop. Place the fabric rectangle between the two sides of the binding. Sew together, gathering.

4 Place each side on its felt lining, then place them right sides facing in while inserting the binding, passing through the decorative handle. Pin the four layers together. Sew the top section between the cut-outs for the spout and handle.

5 On the right side, sew a binding around each cut-out. Turn over and sew on the reverse. Close up the sides and sew binding all around the bottom.

Lampshade

Supplies
Shade covered with fabric, unbleached linen, beads, fabric glue.

1 Embroider the design of your choice on the linen. Cut all around, leaving some extra space around the design. Glue this decoration to the shade.

2 Glue or sew the braid to the top of the shade and the beads to the bottom.

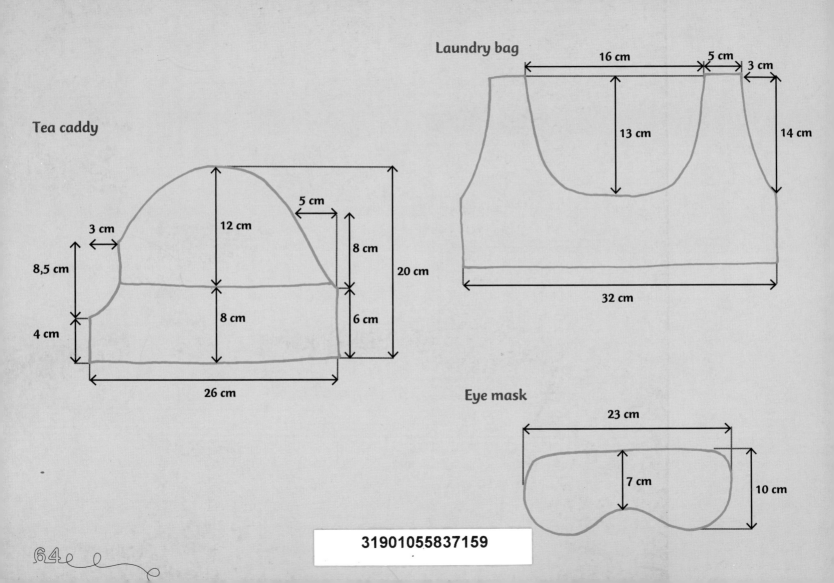

Tea caddy

3 cm

8,5 cm

4 cm

12 cm

5 cm

8 cm

8 cm

6 cm

20 cm

26 cm

Laundry bag

16 cm

5 cm

3 cm

13 cm

14 cm

32 cm

Eye mask

23 cm

7 cm

10 cm

64

31901055837159